CONTENTS

CURRICULUM LINKS … 2

CHARACTER LIST AND STAGING … 4

SCRIPT AND SONG LYRICS … 5

SONGS

1. Lazy Daisy Village … 13
2. Munch, Munch, Munch … 16
3. Big Red Dustbin … 18
4. The Litter Muncher's Dream … 20
5. What A Load Of Rubbish! … 22
6. Sweep In The Morning … 24
7. Happy Machine … 26
8. Big Red Dustbin (Grand Finale) … 30

LICENCE DETAILS … 32

© 2004 Out Of The Ark Music

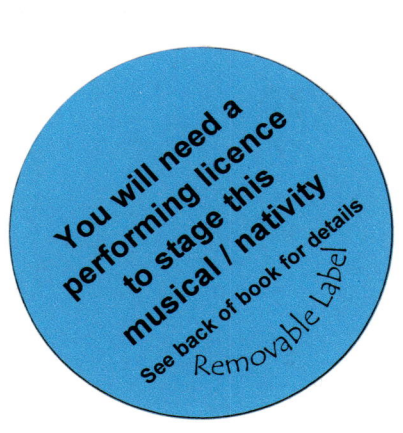

CURRICULUM LINKS

SONG 1 — LAZY DAISY VILLAGE

Knowledge & understanding of the world:

Ask the children to talk about the area in which they live – what they like and dislike about it. Does litter on the roads and pavements make it look better or worse? What other things can the children think of that affect the look of their environment (flower baskets, colourful houses, graffiti, untidy gardens etc).

Talk about the difference between a village and a town.

SONG 2 — MUNCH, MUNCH, MUNCH

Creative development:

Create a 'sound picture' of the Litter Muncher coming down the road and collecting all the rubbish. Find some metal objects to knock together to make the mechanical sounds (spoons, saucepans etc). Add some other classroom instruments, such as triangles, maracas, castanets, tambourines and so on.

Divide all the instruments between the children and begin with just a few, building up more and more instruments as the Litter Muncher comes further down the road collecting litter. As the Litter Muncher passes by and moves away down the road, encourage the children to play more quietly and gradually drop out one by one, until the music fades away completely.

SONG 3 — BIG RED DUSTBIN

Knowledge & understanding of the world:

Talk about how litter is collected from the children's houses. How do the children help in their homes to collect the rubbish and tidy-up?

Talk about recycling rubbish and why this is important in helping protect our environment.

What sorts of rubbish can we recycle? (Paper, glass, cans, textiles, books etc.) Why not set up a 'paper bin' in the classroom that the children can use for their discarded paper and cardboard?

SONG 4 — THE LITTER MUNCHER'S DREAM

Communication, language and literacy:
Talk about dreams and dreaming.

Creative development: Ask the children to draw pictures of the dreams they have had.

SONG 5 — WHAT A LOAD OF RUBBISH!

Personal, social and emotional development:
Have a 'keep my school tidy' campaign. Make a plan together to decide on the best way to do this. Try to incorporate some environmentally friendly ideas.

SONG 6 — SWEEP IN THE MORNING

Physical development: This is a great song for music and movement. Use the following actions to dance along to the song – or make up your own:

One, two, sweep in the morning	Four sweeping actions to left
One, two, sweep in the morning	Four sweeping actions to right
One, two, sweep in the morning	Four sweeping actions to left
And throw it all in the bin, put it in	Make 'throwing' action
Throw it all in the bin	'Throwing' action again

SONG 7 — HAPPY MACHINE

Knowledge & understanding of the world:
The children could design their own village, make a map of it and a model village. They could make up a name for it and decide how many houses they want to have. Do they want trees, flowers, hanging baskets and so on? They could have differently labelled or coloured bins for paper, glass, organic waste etc.

CHARACTER LIST

Narrator Can be read by an adult/older child, or split between a group of pupils.

Litter Muncher The leading part, but with only a few lines to learn. Will need a suitably machine-like costume and the ability to produce good 'munching' and 'snoring' sounds!

Villagers Up to fifteen separate parts, each with a simple line to say – or you could divide these lines between fewer children.

Mayor A child who has an air of authority is perfect for this part! Just three lines to learn.

STAGING

You can chose to keep it simple or really go to town, either way will work well with this simple musical. To give the idea of a 'village', you could use large painted cardboard boxes for the houses and buildings. Make a road between these for the Litter Muncher to ride up and down.

You will need some colourful litter bins dotted about (red, blue, green and yellow) which the children could make by covering some plain bins with coloured paper.

Make the Litter Muncher's costume using a large cardboard box to cover the body (with holes for the neck and arms), and a smaller one for the head (with a hole cut out for the face) – both painted yellow. The children can decorate these boxes however they like – for example using silver foil, crepe and tissue paper, egg cartons, milk tops etc. You could use the book cover for further inspiration!

SCRIPT AND SONG LYRICS

NARRATOR A long time ago, far away, there was a little place called Lazy Daisy Village. It was the most beautiful village you had ever seen. There were lovely trees and lovely flowers, but most of all it was beautiful because all the streets and all the pavements were clean and tidy. There was no litter to be seen anywhere. Every day was a fine day in Lazy Daisy Village.

Song 1. LAZY DAISY VILLAGE

1. In Lazy Daisy Village,
   There are lovely trees to see,
   And everyone is smiling,
   Shaking hands with you and me,
   And it's clean and tidy as a village ever could be.

2. In Lazy Daisy Village,
   Everything is bright and neat,
   The sun is always shining,
   On the Lazy Daisy streets,
   And it's clean and tidy as a village ever could be.

3. In Lazy Daisy Village,
   There are lovely trees to see,
   And everyone is smiling,
   Shaking hands with you and me,
   And it's clean and tidy as a village ever could be.

© 2004 Out of the Ark Music, Surrey KT12 4RQ

NARRATOR Now Lazy Daisy Village was clean and tidy for a reason. Everyday a little machine came chugging along. The little machine was called the Litter Muncher. He was bright yellow and he made lots of friendly clanking and buzzing and whirring noises. And as he went along he munched up all the rubbish. He munched and munched until it had all disappeared and Lazy Daisy Village was bright and tidy again.

Song 2. MUNCH, MUNCH, MUNCH

1. Here comes the Litter Muncher,
   He's a busy machine.
   Here comes the Litter Muncher,
   Keeping everything clean,
   Keeping everything clean,
   Munch, munch, munch,
   Munch, munch, munch, munch.

2. Here comes the Litter Muncher,
   He is always our friend.
   Here comes the Litter Muncher,
   On him, we can depend,
   On him, we can depend,
   Munch, munch, munch,
   Munch, munch, munch, munch.

3. Here comes the Litter Muncher,
   He's a busy machine.
   Here comes the Litter Muncher,
   Keeping everything clean,
   Keeping everything clean,
   Munch, munch, munch,
   Munch, munch, munch, munch.

© 2004 Out of the Ark Music, Surrey KT12 4RQ

NARRATOR There were lots of dustbins in the village, big bins in different colours. There were red bins and blue bins and green bins and yellow bins. But nobody ever put any rubbish in them. All the people just threw it down and left the Litter Muncher to pick it up. You see, the people of Lazy Daisy Village were rather lazy. It was much easier to drop their rubbish on the ground rather than wait to find a bin to put it in.

Song 3. BIG RED DUSTBIN

1. There's a big *red* dustbin in our street,
In our street, in our street.
There's a big red dustbin in our street,
But we don't put the litter in, oh no!
We don't put the litter in.

2. There's a big *blue* dustbin in our street,
In our street, in our street.
There's a big red dustbin in our street,
But we don't put the litter in, oh no!
We don't put the litter in.

3. There's a big *green* dustbin in our street …

4. There's a big *yellow* dustbin in our street …

© 2004 Out of the Ark Music, Surrey KT12 4RQ

NARRATOR Everyday the people dropped more and more rubbish and the Litter Muncher worked harder and harder. He began to feel very tired and he hoped that the villagers would help.

LITTER MUNCHER Please could you put some of your rubbish in the bin?

VILLAGER 1 Oh, I really can't be bothered!

LITTER MUNCHER But I feel very tired.

VILLAGER 2 I'm much too busy to find a bin!

VILLAGER 3 It's *your* job, Litter Muncher!

NARRATOR The Litter Muncher got so tired that one day he had no energy left at all. He sat down, rubbed his eyes, lay down on the village green and went to sleep. While he was asleep he had a lovely dream, where everyone in Lazy Daisy Village put all their rubbish into the big coloured bins.

Song 4. THE LITTER MUNCHER'S DREAM

1   The Litter Muncher had a dream,
    Had a dream, had a dream,
    The Litter Muncher had a dream,
    And all on a summer's day,
    All on a summer's day.

2   The people kept their village clean,
    Village clean, village clean,
    The people kept their village clean,
    And all on a summer's day,
    All on a summer's day.

3   They put their litter in the bins,
    In the bins, in the bins,
    They put their litter in the bins,
    And all on a summer's day,
    All on a summer's day.

4   And it was such a lovely dream,
    Lovely dream, lovely dream,
    And it was such a lovely dream,
    And all on a summer's day,
    All on a summer's day.

© 2004 Out of the Ark Music, Surrey KT12 4RQ

NARRATOR   The villagers saw that the Litter Muncher was asleep, so they tried to wake him up.

VILLAGER 4   Litter Muncher, Litter Muncher, wake up!

LITTER MUNCHER   Snore!

VILLAGER 5   We need you to collect the rubbish!

LITTER MUNCHER   Snore!

VILLAGER 6   Our village will get untidy!

LITTER MUNCHER   Snore!

NARRATOR   But they couldn't wake the Litter Muncher up.

VILLAGER 7   What's going to happen to the rubbish now?

VILLAGER 8   Should we put it in the bins?

Villagers all think for a moment, then shake their heads

ALL VILLAGERS   No, no! We can't be bothered!

NARRATOR   For days, the Litter Muncher slept and the days turned into weeks. The villagers kept dropping their litter on the pavements and the streets and all over the village green. Everyday there was more and more until there were great big piles of rubbish everywhere. It looked horrible and it was *very* smelly!

                            The villagers didn't like the rubbish.

VILLAGER 9   Our village is so untidy!

VILLAGER 10   It's not a beautiful village anymore.

VILLAGER 11   The rubbish looks horrible!

ALL VILLAGERS   And it's SO smelly!! Uhhrrr!!!

Song 5. WHAT A LOAD OF RUBBISH!

1. What a load of rubbish,
    What a horrible sight!
    Our lovely village used to be alright.
    Loads of banana skins smelling grim,
    We wish that we'd put our litter in the bins!

2. What a load of rubbish,
    What a horrible sight!
    Our lovely village used to be alright.
    Loads of yoghurt pots smelling grim,
    We wish that we'd put our litter in the bins!

3. What a load of rubbish,
    What a horrible sight!
    Our lovely village used to be alright.
    Fish and chips wrappers smelling grim,
    We wish that we'd put our litter in the bins!

© 2004 Out of the Ark Music, Surrey KT12 4RQ

NARRATOR One day, the Lady/Lord Mayor came to visit Lazy Daisy Village. S/he looked at the rubbish and held her/his nose.

MAYOR What a mess!!

NARRATOR The Mayor called out to the villagers.

MAYOR Go and get your sweeping brushes!

NARRATOR So everyone went to get a sweeping brush.

MAYOR Now, sweep up all this mess!

NARRATOR Nobody argued with the Mayor because s/he was very bossy!

So the villagers swept and swept and swept up the rubbish.

Song 6. SWEEP IN THE MORNING

1. One, two, sweep in the morning,
   One, two, sweep in the morning,
   One, two, sweep in the morning,
   And throw it all in the bin, put it in,
   And throw it all in the bin!

2. Three, four, sweep in the afternoon,
   Three, four, sweep in the afternoon,
   Three, four, sweep in the afternoon,
   And throw it all in the bin, put it in,
   And throw it all in the bin!

3. Five, six, sweep after teatime,
   Five, six, sweep after teatime,
   Five, six, sweep after teatime,
   And throw it all in the bin, put it in,
   And throw it all in the bin!

4. Seven, eight, sweep in the evening,
   Seven, eight, sweep in the evening,
   Seven, eight, sweep in the evening,
   And throw it all in the bin, put it in,
   And throw it all in the bin!

5 Nine, ten, sweep up the litter,
   Nine, ten, sweep up the litter,
   Nine, ten, sweep up the litter,
   And throw it all in the bin, put it in,
   And throw it all in the bin!

   Yeah!

   © 2004 Out of the Ark Music, Surrey KT12 4RQ

NARRATOR It took three whole days to tidy up Lazy Daisy Village and everyone felt very tired.

VILLAGER 12 Poor Litter Muncher! Now we know how he must feel!

NARRATOR The villagers went and woke up the Litter Muncher.

VILLAGER 13 Please wake up Litter Muncher.

VILLAGER 14 We're really very sorry.

VILLAGER 15 From now on we're going to put all our rubbish in the bins.

NARRATOR The Litter Muncher was SO pleased that he didn't have to work as hard any more. All he ever had to do was empty the bins and munch up the fallen leaves in the autumn. He was such a happy Litter Muncher.

Song 7. HAPPY MACHINE

1 Hey, Litter Muncher, chugging along,
   You're a happy machine,
   Because all the people around,
   Help you keep things clean,
   And Lazy Daisy Village,
   Is the cleanest ever seen.

2 Hey, Litter Muncher chugging along,
   Having a lovely day.
   Everyone is waving at you,
   As they go on their way,
   And all the litter goes in the bins,
   Every single day.

3   Hey, Litter Muncher, chugging along,
    You're a happy machine,
    Because all the people around,
    Help you keep things clean,
    And Lazy Daisy Village,
    Is the cleanest ever seen.

© 2004 Out of the Ark Music, Surrey KT12 4RQ

NARRATOR From that moment on, all the villagers put their rubbish in the bins. And as the sun rose for another beautiful day, everyone felt very happy to live in such a clean and tidy village.

Song 8. BIG RED DUSTBIN (Grand Finale)

1   There's a big *red* dustbin in our street,
    In our street, in our street.
    There's a big red dustbin in our street,
    And we all put the litter in, we do!
    We all put the litter in.

2   There's a big *blue* dustbin in our street,
    In our street, in our street.
    There's a big red dustbin in our street,
    And we all put the litter in, we do!
    We all put the litter in.

3   There's a big *green* dustbin in our street …

4   There's a big *yellow* dustbin in our street …

© 2004 Out of the Ark Music, Surrey KT12 4RQ

Lazy Daisy Village

Words & Music by
Niki Davies

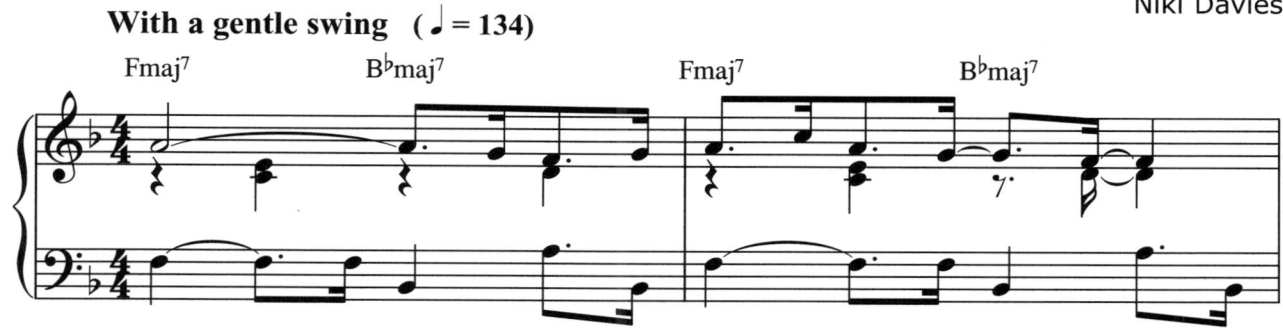

© 2004 Out of the Ark Music, Surrey KT12 4RQ

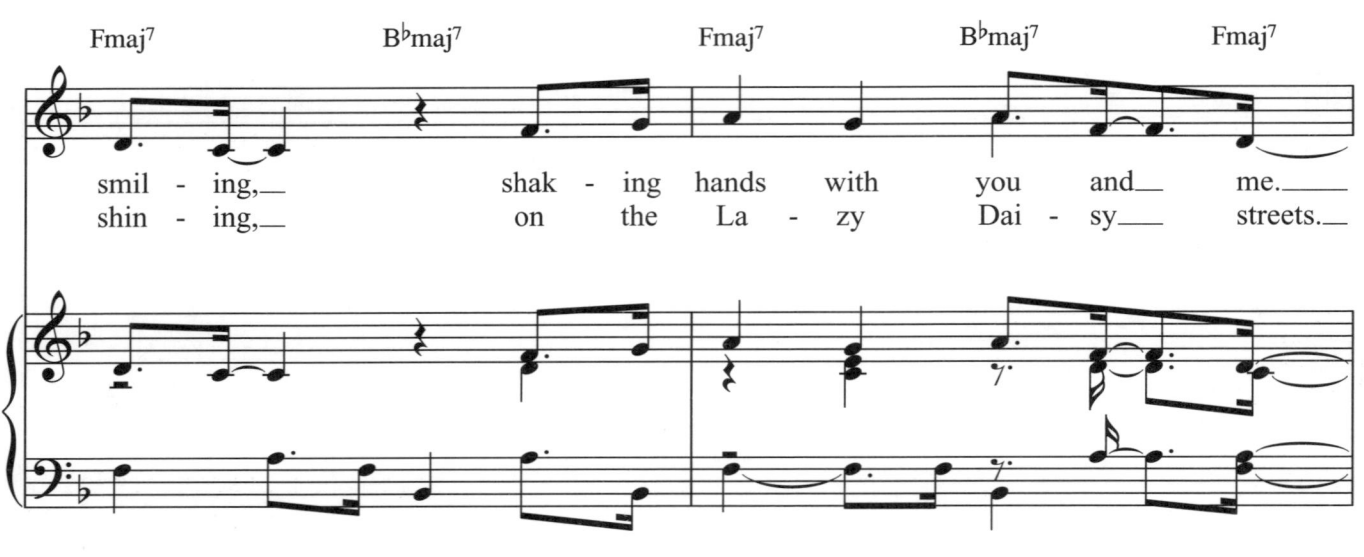
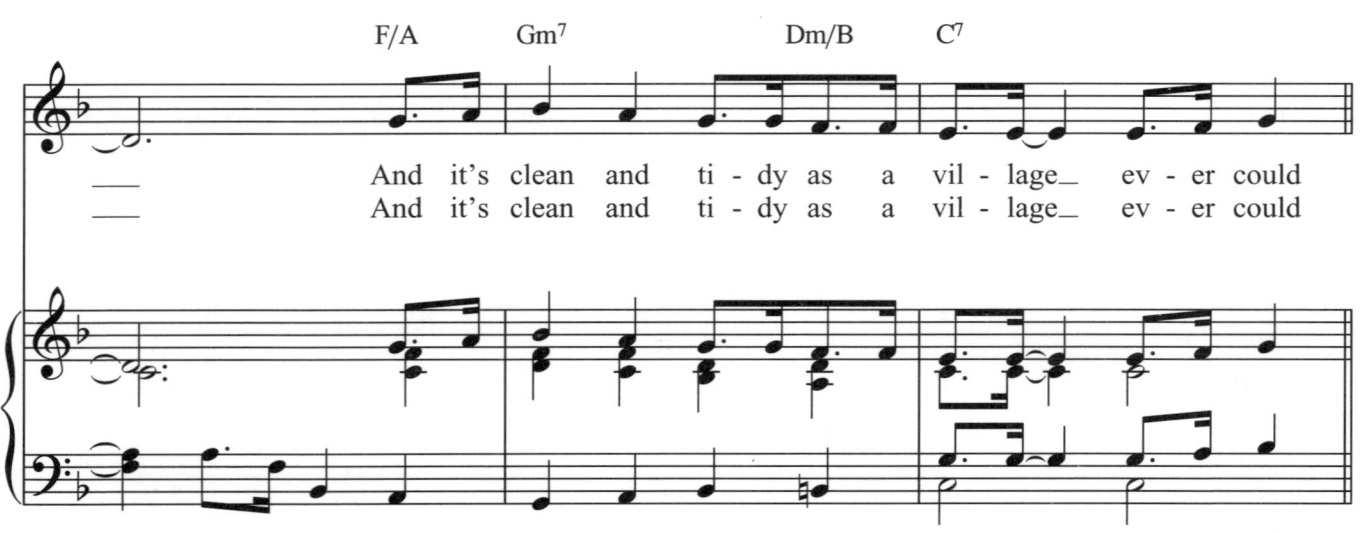

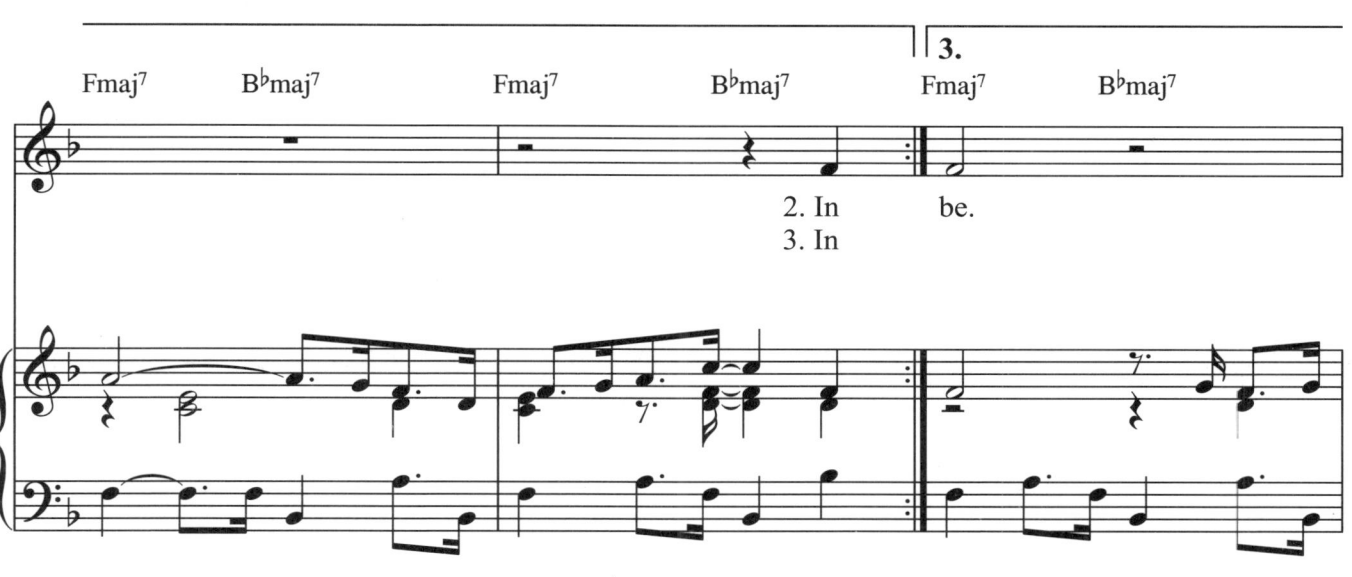

Munch, Munch, Munch

Words & Music by
Niki Davies

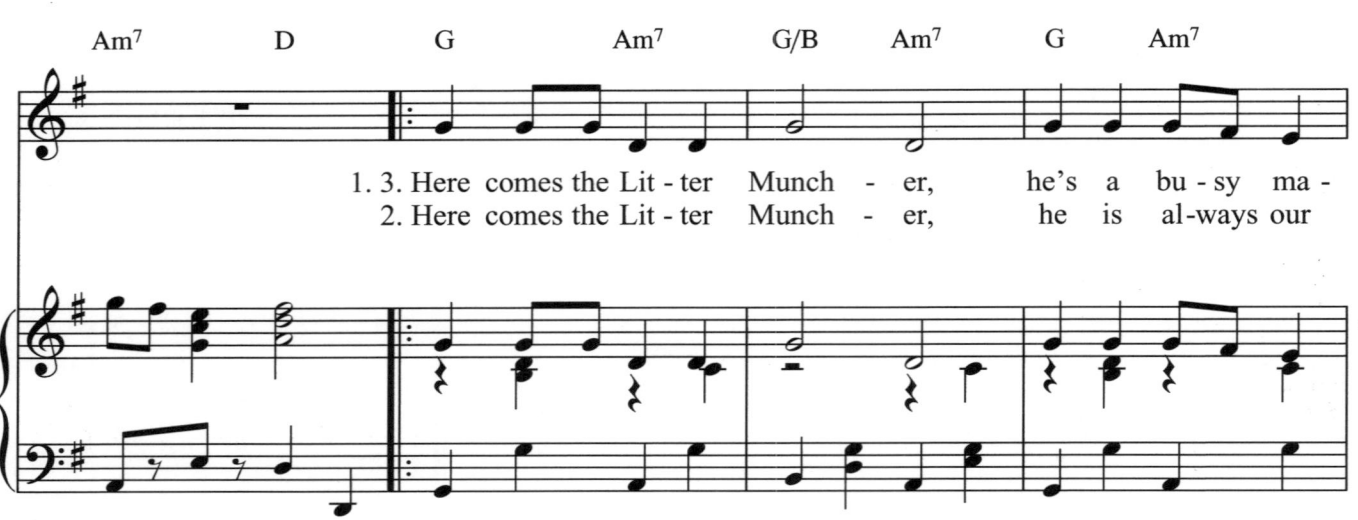

1.3. Here comes the Lit-ter Munch-er, he's a bu-sy ma-
2. Here comes the Lit-ter Munch-er, he is al-ways our

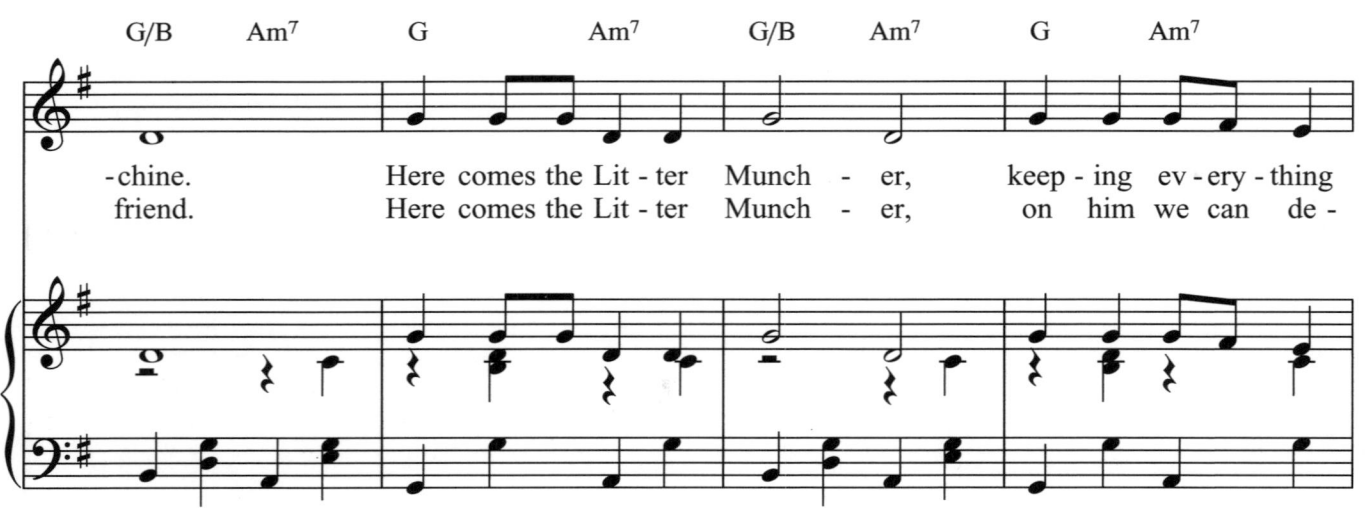

-chine. Here comes the Lit-ter Munch-er, keep-ing ev-ery-thing
friend. Here comes the Lit-ter Munch-er, on him we can de-

© 2004 Out of the Ark Music, Surrey KT12 4RQ

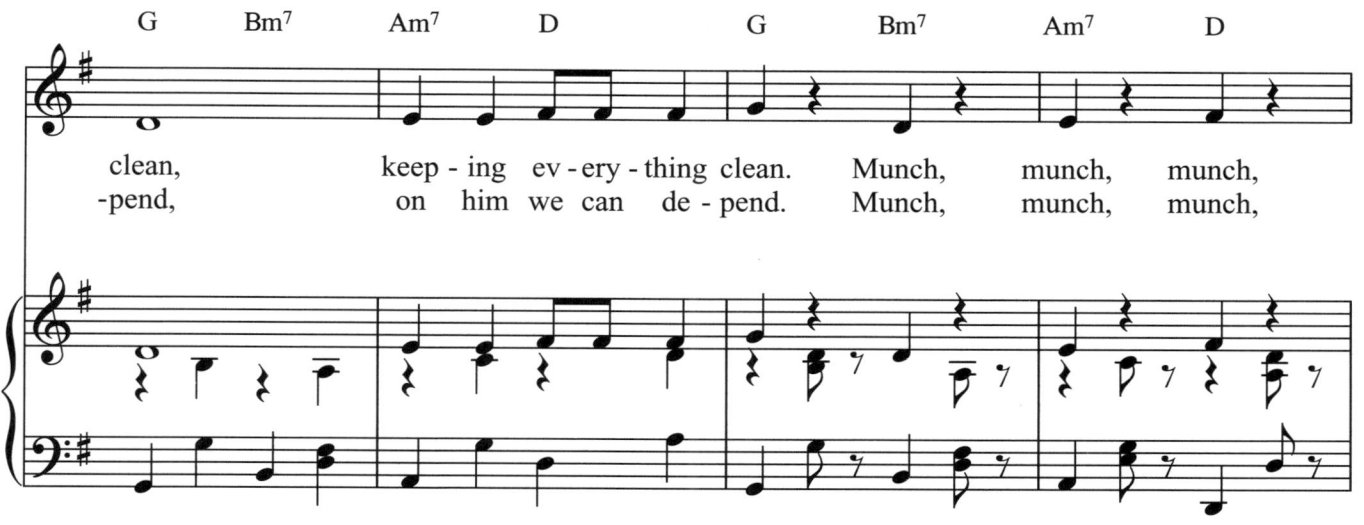

Big Red Dustbin

Words & Music by
Niki Davies

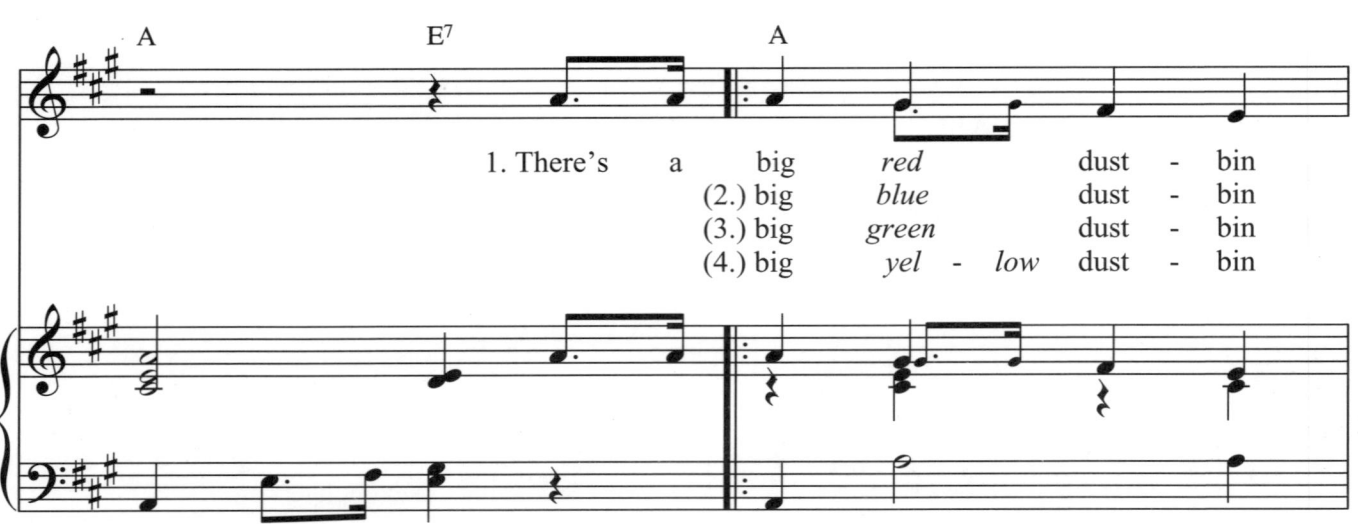

1. There's a big *red* dust-bin
(2.) big *blue* dust-bin
(3.) big *green* dust-bin
(4.) big *yel-low* dust-bin

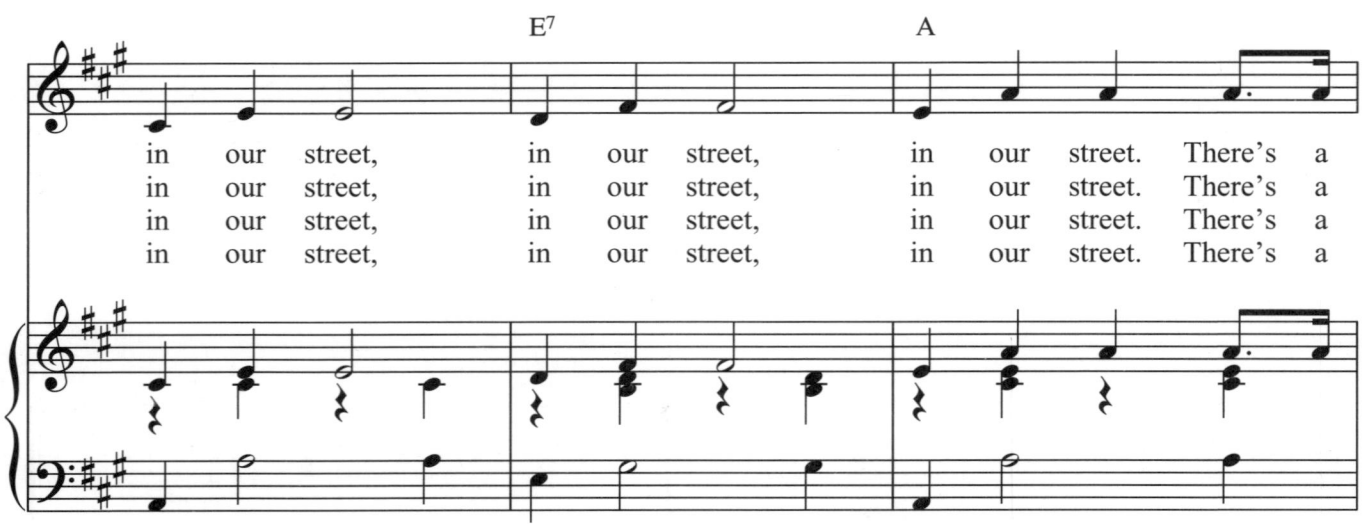

in our street, in our street, in our street. There's a
in our street, in our street, in our street. There's a
in our street, in our street, in our street. There's a
in our street, in our street, in our street. There's a

© 2004 Out of the Ark Music, Surrey KT12 4RQ

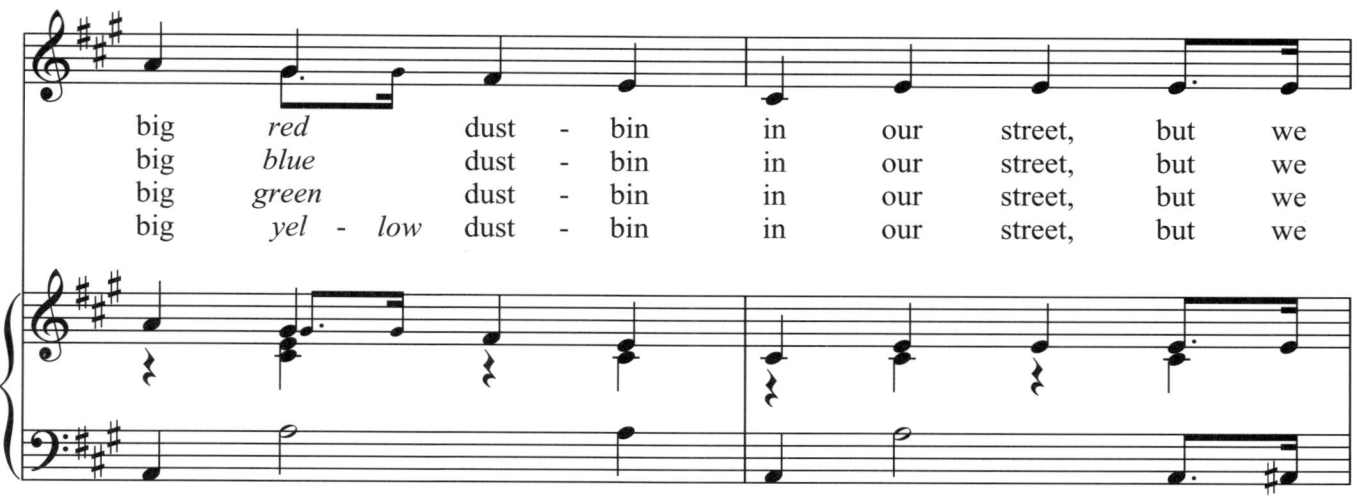
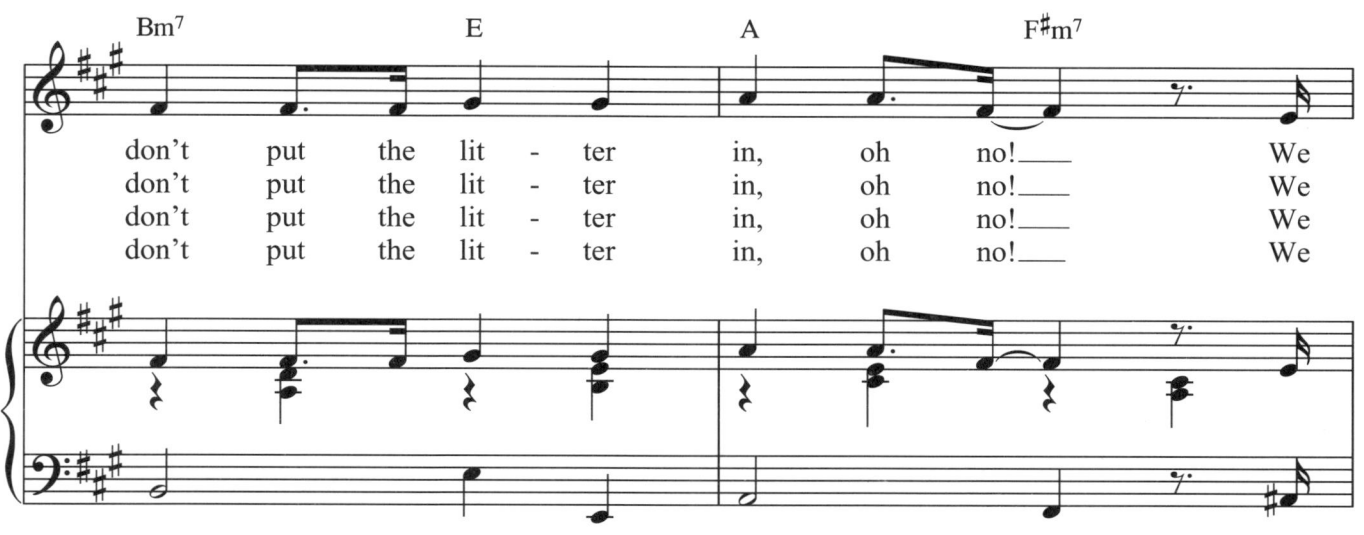

The Litter Muncher's Dream

Words & Music by
Niki Davies

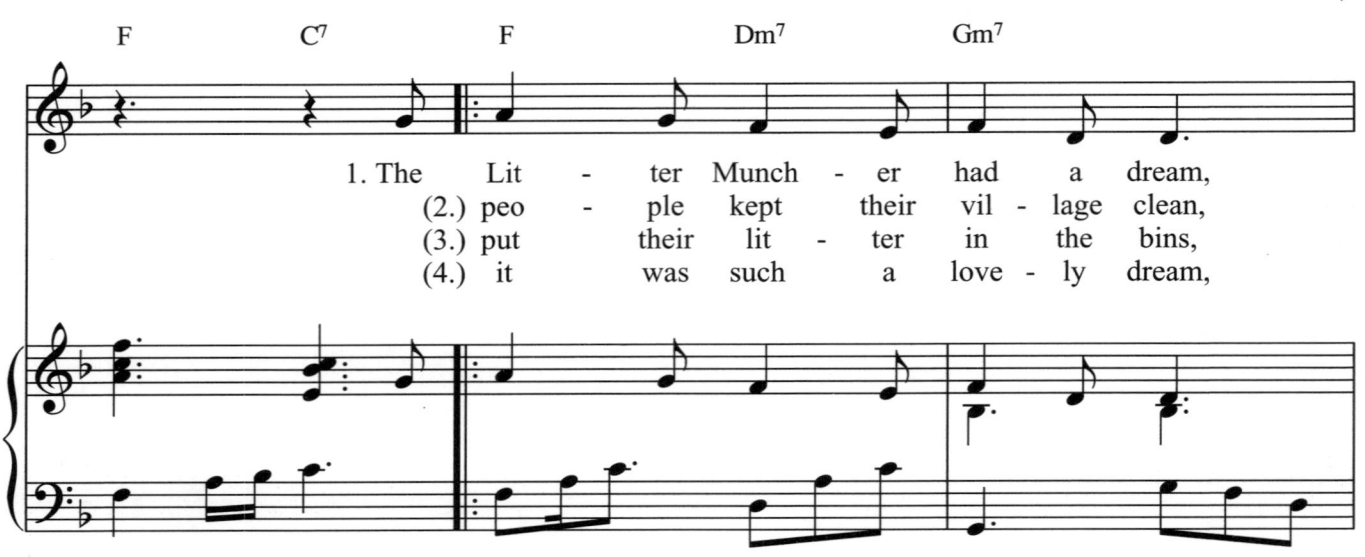

© 2004 Out of the Ark Music, Surrey KT12 4RQ

What A Load Of Rubbish!

Words & Music by
Niki Davies

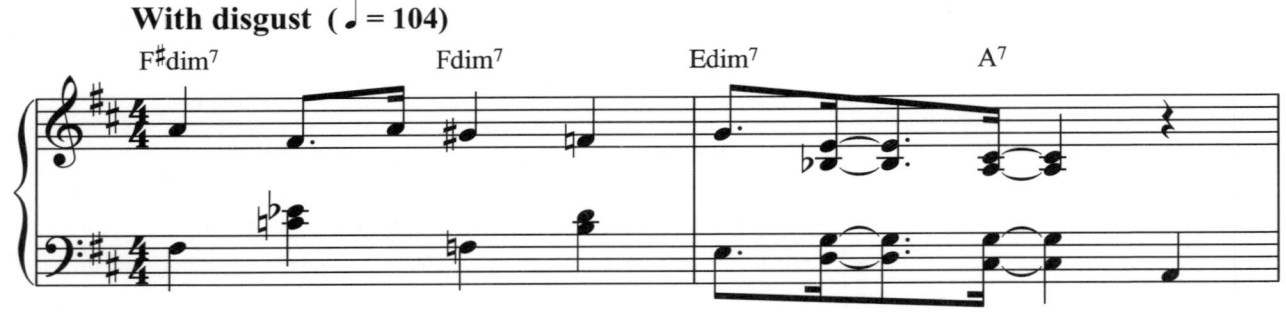

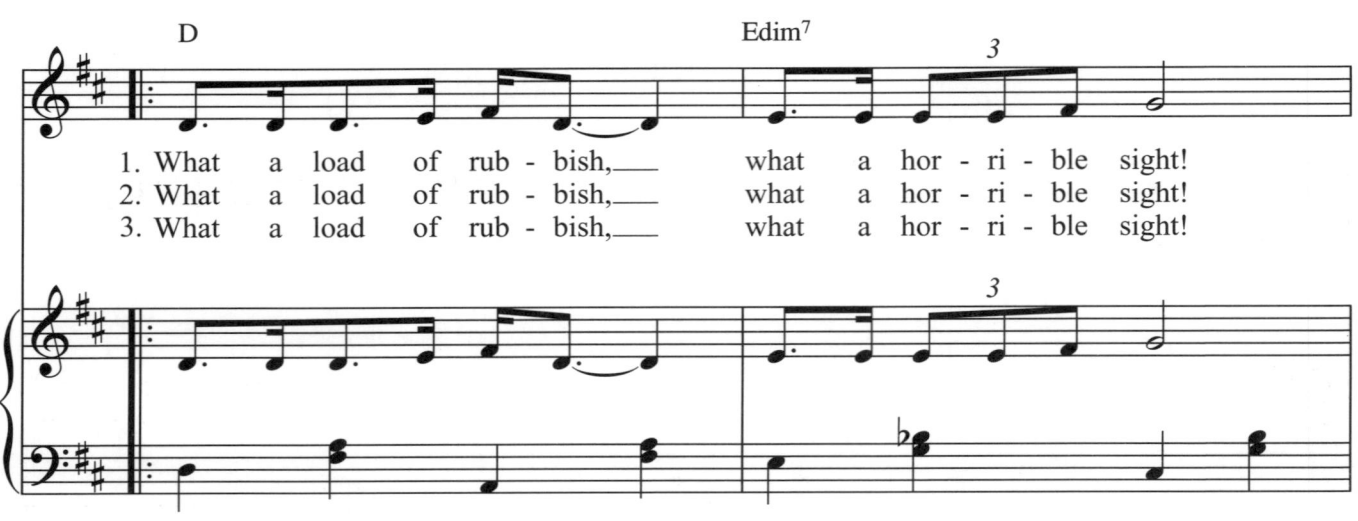

1. What a load of rub-bish,___ what a hor-ri-ble sight!
2. What a load of rub-bish,___ what a hor-ri-ble sight!
3. What a load of rub-bish,___ what a hor-ri-ble sight!

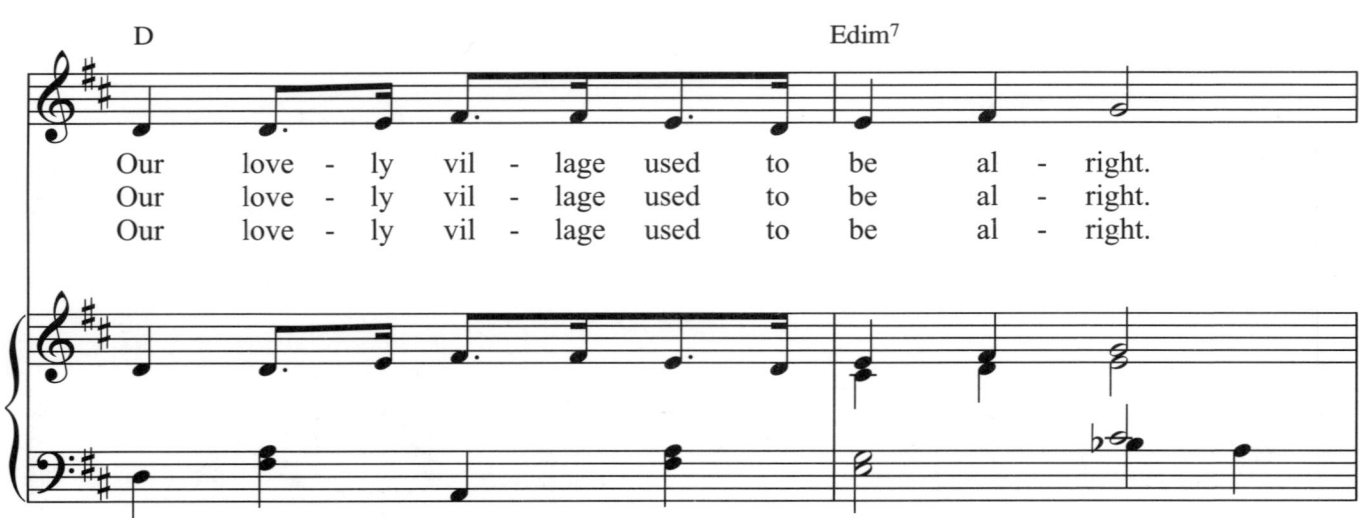

Our love-ly vil-lage used to be al-right.
Our love-ly vil-lage used to be al-right.
Our love-ly vil-lage used to be al-right.

© 2004 Out of the Ark Music, Surrey KT12 4RQ

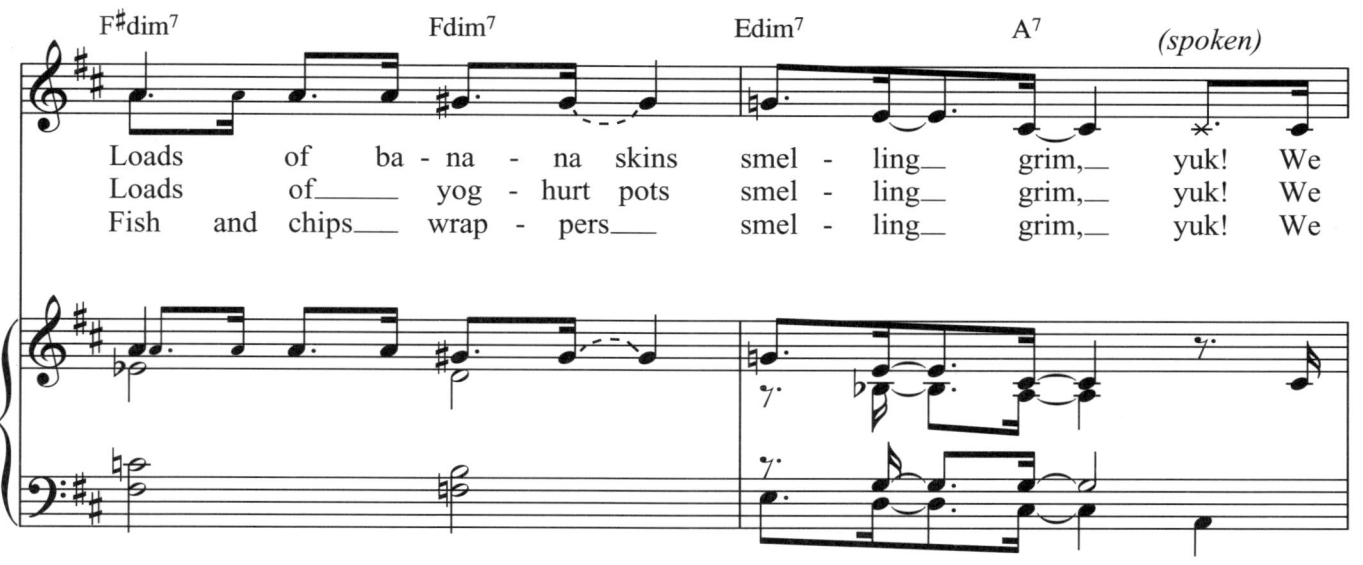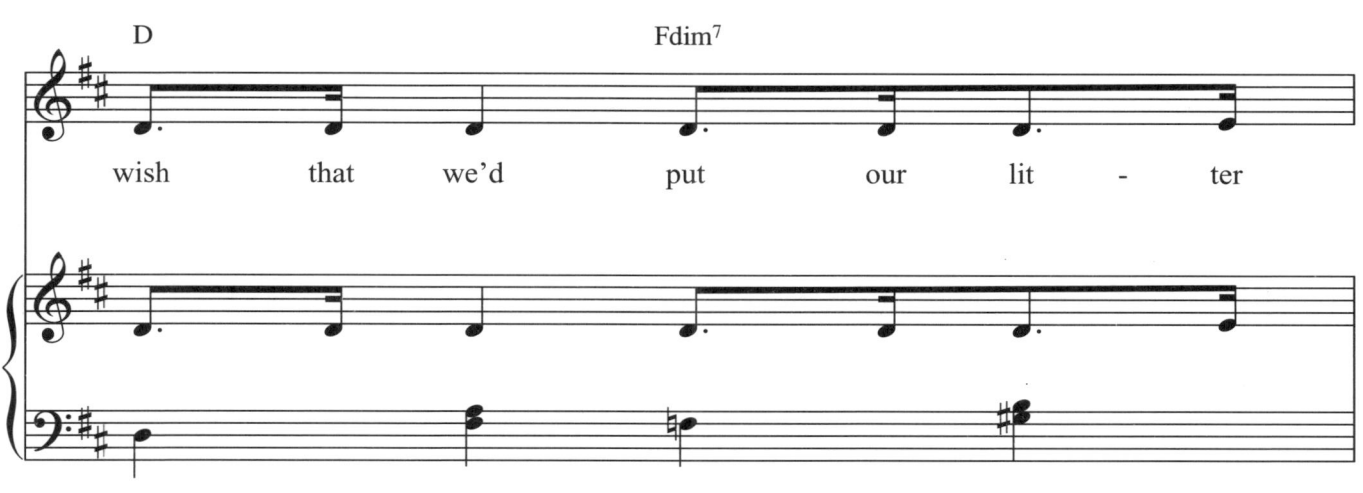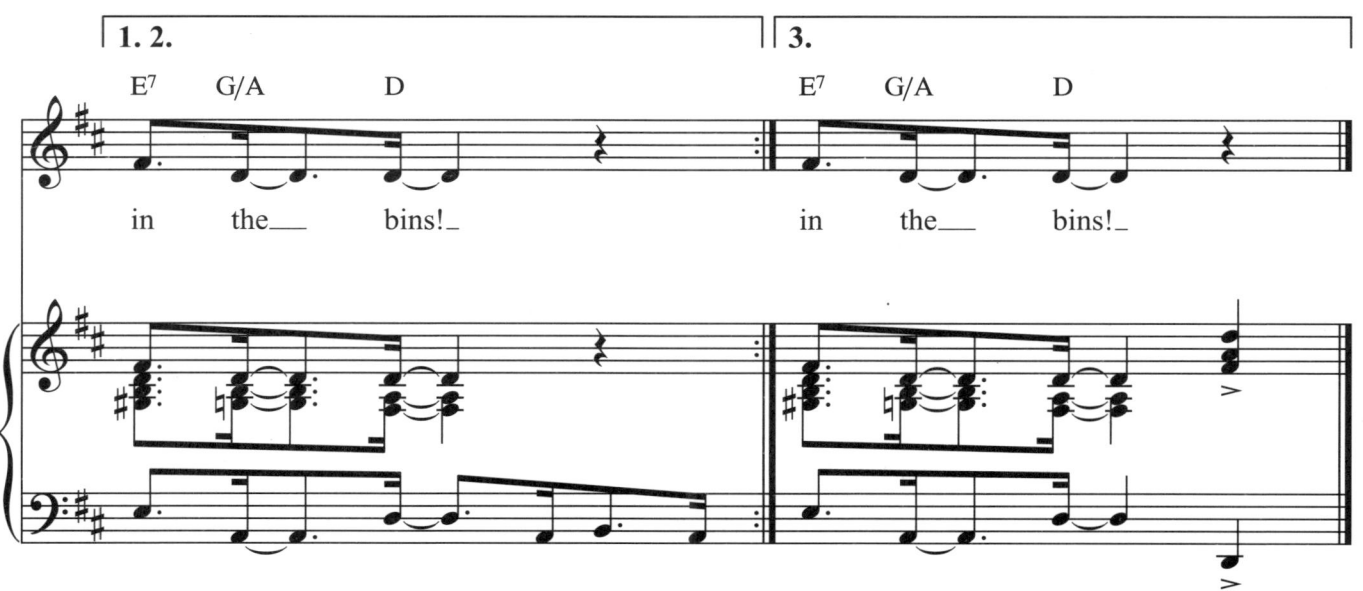

Sweep In The Morning

Words & Music by
Niki Davies

Happy Machine

Words & Music by
Niki Davies

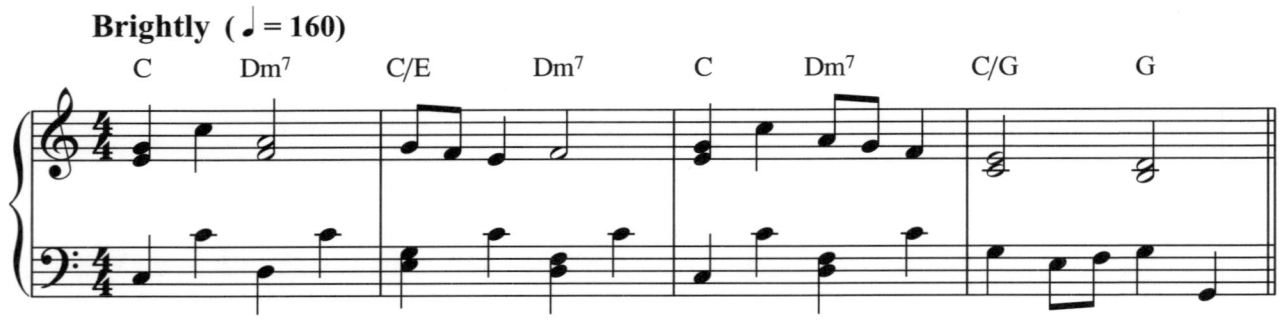
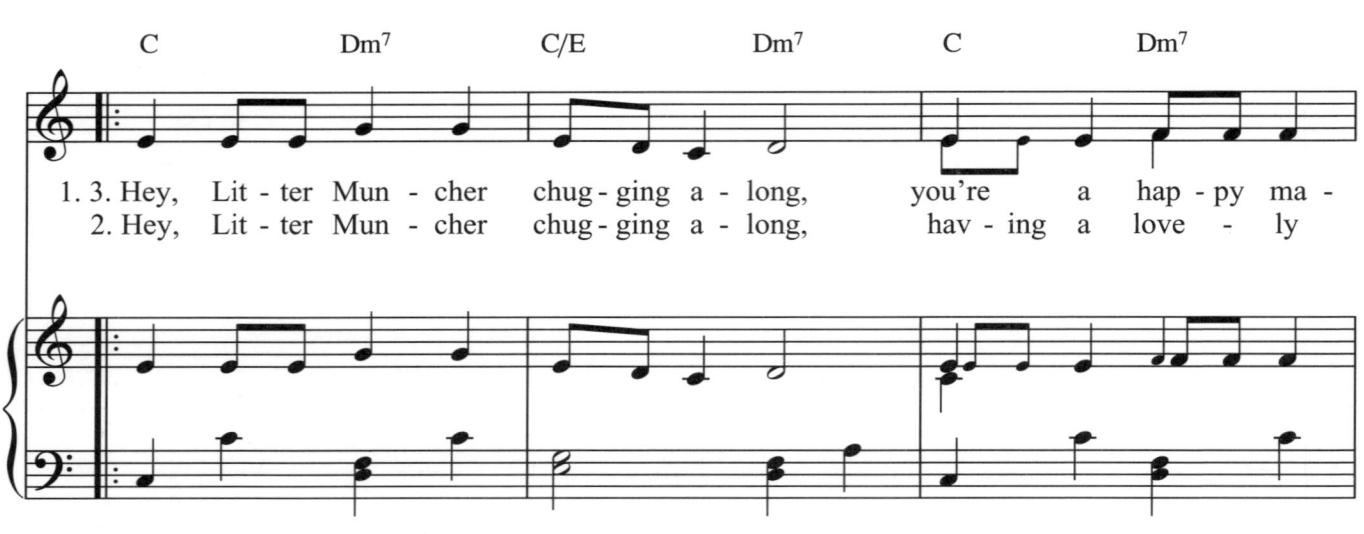
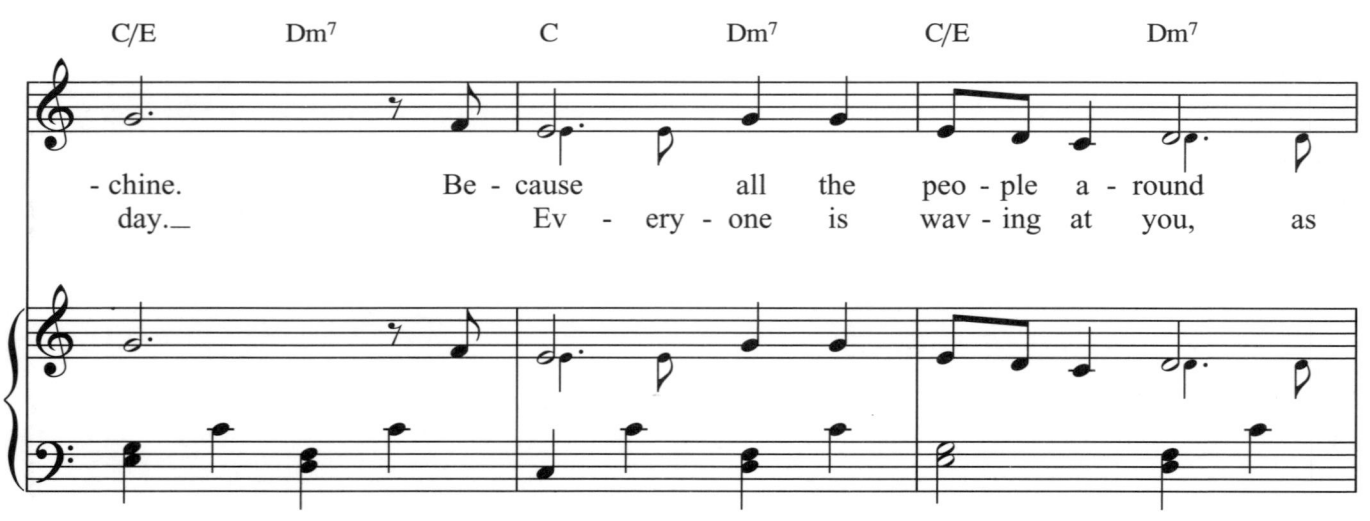

© 2004 Out of the Ark Music, Surrey KT12 4RQ

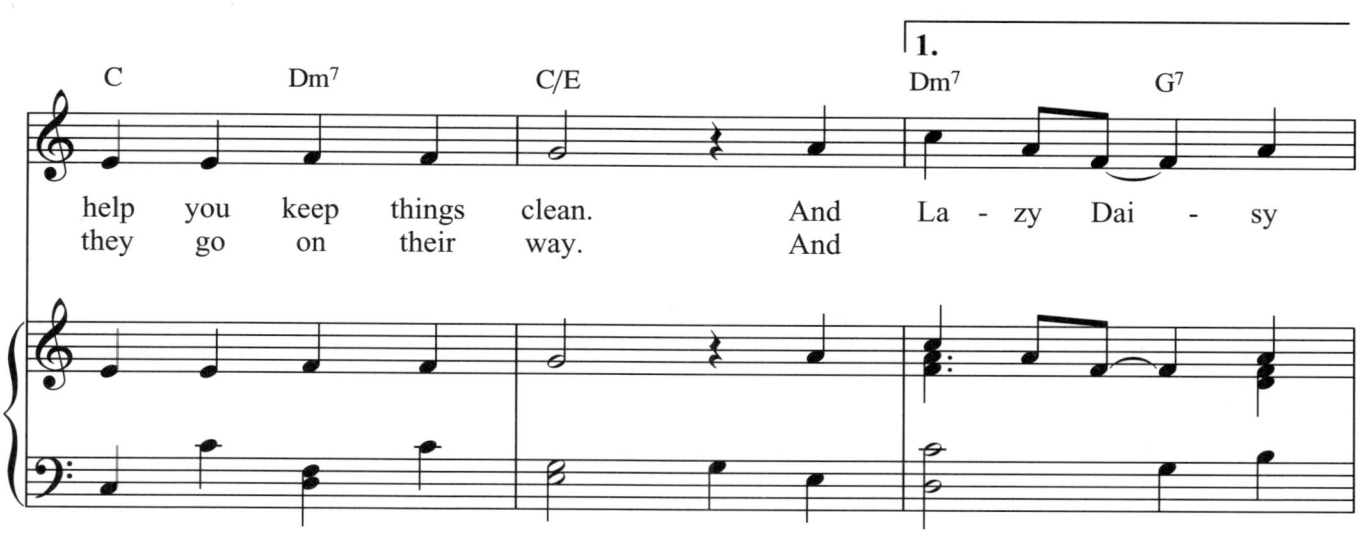
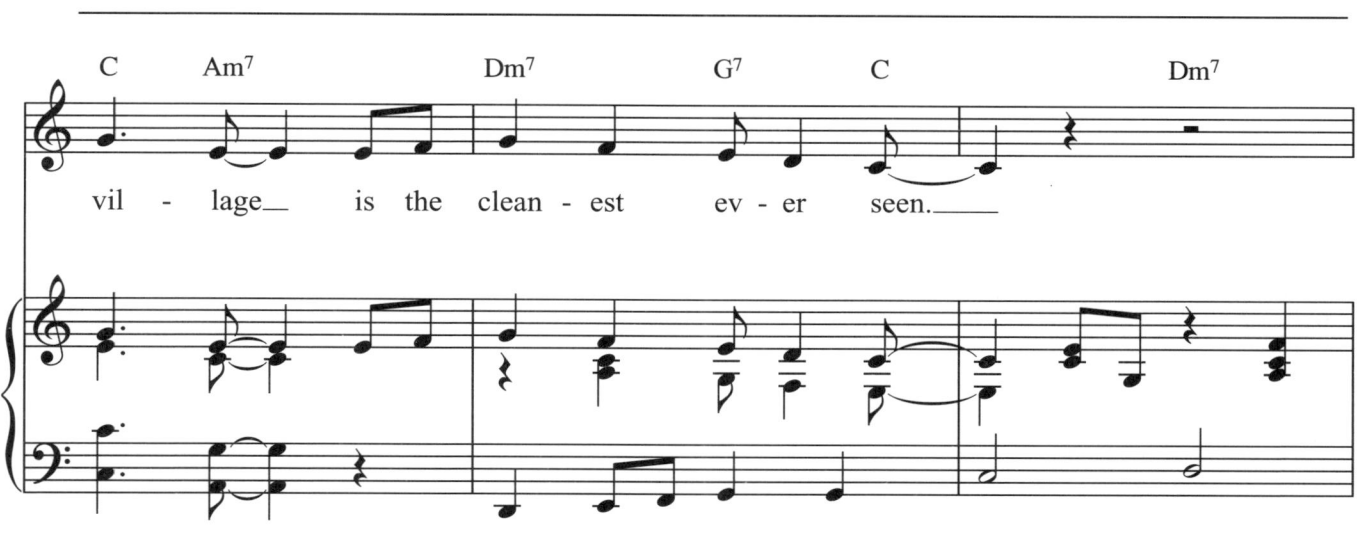

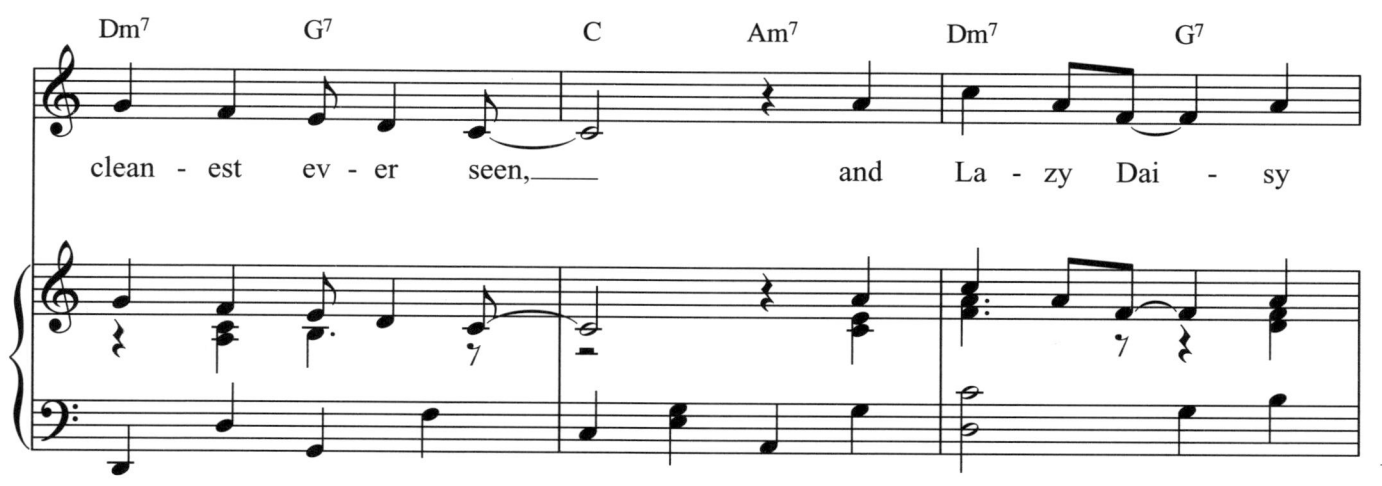

Big Red Dustbin
(Grand Finale)

Words & Music by
Niki Davies

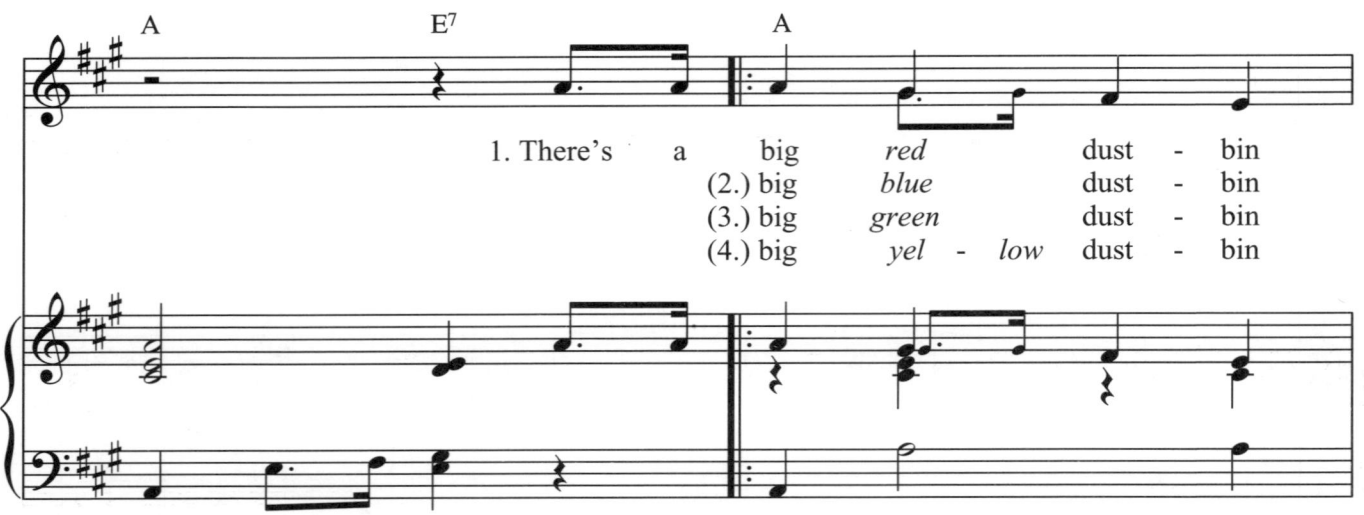
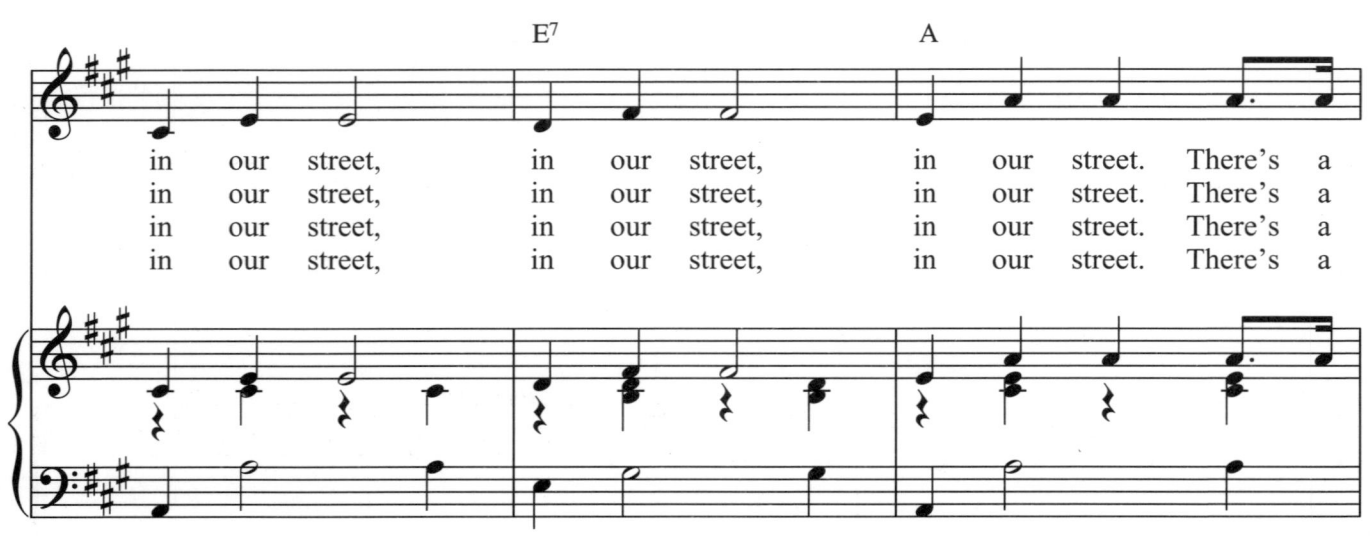

© 2004 Out of the Ark Music, Surrey KT12 4RQ

(UK / EIRE / EU)* LICENCE APPLICATION FORM

*To stage this play in non-EU countries please contact Out of the Ark Music for an alternative form.

If you perform The Litter Muncher to an audience other than children and staff you will need to photocopy and complete this form and return it by post or fax to Out of the Ark Music in order to apply for a licence. *If anticipated audience sizes are very small or if special circumstances apply please contact us*.

We wish to apply for a licence to perform 'The Litter Muncher' by Niki Davies

Customer number (if known): ....

Name of school / organisation: ....

Name of organiser / producer: ....

Date(s) of performance(s): ....

Invoice address: ....
....
....
....

Post code: .... Country: ....

Telephone number: ....

Number of performances (excl. dress rehearsal) | **Performances without admission charges** | **Performances with admission charges**

1 ☐ £11.75* (inc VAT) ☐ £18.80* (inc VAT)

2 ☐ £18.80* (inc VAT) ☐ £23.50* (inc VAT)

Tick one of the boxes above. For 3 or more performances contact Out of the Ark Music for details.

Tick one of the three payment options below: *(Invoices will be sent with all licences)*

☐ Please bill me / my school or nursery at the above address

☐ I enclose a cheque (pounds sterling) for £   payable to **Out of the Ark Music**

☐ Please charge the following card: (VISA, MasterCard and American Express accepted)

| Card no: | | Expiry date: | _ _ / _ _ (MM/YY) |

If the performance is to be recorded in order to sell the recording to parents or to the public please contact Out of the Ark Music. We convey to the licence holder the right to reproduce printed lyrics of the songs in programmes distributed to the audience. The following credit should be included with the lyrics: *'Reproduced by kind permission. © Out of the Ark Music'*

Address: Out of the Ark Music   Phone: +44 (0)1932 232 250
           Sefton House   Fax: +44 (0)1932 703 010
           2 Molesey Road   Email: info@outoftheark.com
           Hersham Green
           Walton-on-Thames
           Surrey KT12 4RQ
           United Kingdom

*The licence fees shown on this form are for 2004–2005 and may be subject to revision.